FEASTING ON SKY
poems by eric morago

Published by Paper Plane Pilot Publishing
Los Angeles, California
www.thepaperplanepilots.com

Copyright © 2016, Eric Morago. All Rights Reserved.

All content contained in this book is the intellectual property of Eric Morago and may not be copied, reproduced, distributed or displayed without Eric Morago's express written permission. For information e-mail Paper Plane Pilot Publishing at thepaperplanepilots@gmail.com

Edited by Anthony Khayat, Alisha Attella, Nancy Lynée Woo & Danielle Mitchell

Cover Art by Gabriel Chavez
Cover Design by Laura Khayat
Interior Art by Laura Khayat
Interior Design by Sara Khayat
Author Photo by Boris Ingles

Proofread by Michael J. Hetzler & Jim Hoggatt

ISBN-13: 978-0-9979836-1-6
ISBN-10: 0-9979836-1-2

This copy is a first edition.

for Nicholas

CONTENTS

Unfastened	11

i.

Reverse	15
Inheritance	16
The First Step in Treating Mental Illness	20
What I Think About When I Am Bench-Pressing More Weight Than I Probably Should Without a Spotter	22
Outstanding	23
This Poem Isn't Very Good, but in an Alternate Universe Somewhere There's a Version of It That's Much Better	24
Real Hunger	25
First Kill	27
Second Coming, Pride Parade	30

ii.

What I Said to the Ghost	33
First Session	34
Why I Wore a Magnetic Earring in the 7th Grade	36
The Girl in My Poetry Class	38
Velcro	40
For What It's Worth	41
Sunset	42
Expanding Universe Theory	43
The World Was Supposed to End Yesterday	46
Tiny Bones of Youth, Lost	48

iii.

Homecoming Dance	55
On the Night of My Ten-Year Reunion	58
Against Better Judgment	59
Like a Hot Knife Through Butter	61
Private Dance	63
4 Haiku	65
I Don't Like Straws	66
Smolder	67
Coveting the Man Covered in Burns	69
Home Remedy	70
Playing the Game *Would You Rather*, You Ask	71

iv.

Surviving a Mountain Lion Attack, As Instructed by eHow.com	75
Intangible	77
How You Spend Your Summer Vacation	80
Squeeze	83
Free Association	84
When My Therapist Shares His Poetry with Me	86
Priorities	89
Starstuff	90
One Man's Trainwreck Is Another's Golden Goose	92

v.

Confessions of a Retiring Magician	95
You're a Good Zombie, Charlie Brown	96
For All Intense and Porpoises, This Poem Is a Mistake	98
She Calls It Wasteful When I Leave Food on My Plate, and I Call It Politics	99
Bigfoot's To-Do List	101
The Silver Bridge	103
From the Loch, to the Monster	105

Controlled Crash	106
3 Billion Beats	108
The First Time I Saw Snow Fall Was Also the Only Time I Ever	110
Acknowledgments	113

*Monsters are real, and ghosts are real too.
They live inside us, and sometimes, they win.*

—*Stephen King*

UNFASTENED
for the 101-year-old woman who paraglided for her birthday

When they fastened the harness, explained
its aerodynamics, the means by which you'd fly,
did you imagine it'd come that easy to your bones—
how the arthritis would chip away like chiseled rock,
leave you so weightless birds believed you goddess?
Before you became a one-hundred-and-one-year-old
firework show, had you already known your body
was built for the sky—your skin always wind-chimed
song? Look at you now, hanging in the air like a wish.
You are so free, it is as if you divorced gravity, slipped
the wedding band off like a straitjacket and put on
your best-looking dress—one that makes the roaring
20's come alive in your chest again, where the band
plays into early morning and your dance is a climb
in altitude. We cannot help but marvel your flight—
its record-breaking reminder how our years do not
have to anchor us to this earth, how all our bodies
can refuse physics and the cruel principles of time.
Thank you for this gift—your promise we are each
our own miracle, suspended below a hollow fabric
wing of hope. How if we'd just let go, unfastened
from all this disbelief, we would not fall.

i.

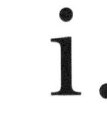

REVERSE

We were reverse alchemy. Gold
changed back to lead. Our hearts,
a pair of origami cranes, unfolded
paper once again. The language
of goodbye devolved to wordless
gesture—a civil nod, then muted
bodies, backwards-turned. Now
I am fish, grown gills and writhe
to find water, to swim, to dive—
to escape the dirt, the earth, you.

INHERITANCE

I.

My grandfather believed in ghosts—
swore, as a child, he saw one once
move through an orange grove
like a wild dog stalking
rabbits in the brush.

He said he knew, that night,
what it was to be haunted.

I thought him blessed and brave
to stare such a spirit down,
to see what so few ever do—
revelation our bodies hide
secrets science can't know.

Six years old and I wondered
if I'd carry his same luck,
inheriting ghost stories
of my own some day.

II.

Years later, a much darker tale—
his father, a drunk, found dead.

No note, just a shotgun
beside the body, smoke

rising from its barrel
                          like a soul.

My grandfather, a young boy,
alone in this discovery,
called out for the others to come—
to pull him back into himself.

Waiting, he told me how hard
it was to keep from looking up.
Specks of skull and other bits
spread out like stars.

Their dizzy red pattern—
astrology he feared
would follow in his blood.

III.

He was 78 when he passed away—
two years after his wife,
my grandmother, slipped off
like a slipper from a foot.

*I can still hear her voice
in the kitchen,
strong as her coffee,*

he'd often say, without confessing
whether or not he believed
she were *really* there.

Always a careful man—
he kept such swelling love
silent, spoke even less of loss,

and never owned a gun.

He mourned her by eating
the same frozen dinner
every night.

The dance of undressing a tray
from a box and the cutting
of slits to allow for steam
to escape

became the habit
that got him through the day.

IV.

My father called last week,
like a flag at half-mast, to notify
me of yet another cousin's death.

Addiction, a sharpshooter
that has taken aim and fired
on my family again and again.

When my brother died,
I wonder if he noticed the red
sight over his heart,

        before the bullet.

V.

With every second drink I pour
myself now, and on rare nights,
a third, I know my inheritance.

Ghost stories collect like crows,
nesting behind my ribcage.
Wings fuss against my chest—
they are an anxious murder
of black feathers, cawing

at the static in the air,

        at the hint of a storm.

THE FIRST STEP IN TREATING MENTAL ILLNESS

is to admit to needing professional help—
then seek it out.

So I spend all afternoon obsessing,
combing over my HMO's website
to find what is and is not covered.

And I'm starting to feel a little better

by this idea of unabashed honesty
between myself and a credentialed
stranger—a doctor, trained to listen

and not make me feel crazy

when I say things like:
my skin is a parade of exit doors
I open myself.

And for the first time in a while
the anxiety ballet in my stomach
takes an intermission—

that is until I'm on the phone
with an insurance rep requesting
authorization and he asks:

What is the problem?

The question comes down,
both expected and unexpected
like a guillotine blade—

fast, brutal, clean.
This is not the stranger I wanted—
not the one I'd prepared myself for,
the one who was supposed to

make me feel safe, and maybe
that is why it is most important

I answer him.

WHAT I THINK ABOUT WHEN I AM BENCH-PRESSING MORE WEIGHT THAN I PROBABLY SHOULD WITHOUT A SPOTTER

1. I could die. Right now. Betrayed by my body, muscles giving up, or out, like elevator cables snapping from too many sardining in, despite the load limit warning.

2. Elevators used to cause me a great deal of anxiety. They don't anymore. Only slightly now, and in certain buildings. Usually old ones. That itchy-heart-creature-crawling-in-my-chest sensation I once associated with being pulled and suspended, stories high, by unseen forces in a giant metal tomb has been reassigned to driving on twisty freeway overpasses and the fear I might suddenly turn the wheel too far towards the direction of falling.

3. I know my arms can lift this bar, bring it down to my chest then back up again, five—maybe six—more times, so I wonder what if it's not my body I need to worry about? What if my brain were a traitor—a double agent that when ordered to eliminate its target, did so by making it look like an accident?

4. Could the cables of an elevator car give, not from too much weight, but from being cut?

5. If I were crushed on this bench, pinned by physics and too much mass, how many would come rushing over? And how many would it take to lift that which I could not?

6. Pancaked lungs probably sound a lot like whoopee cushions playing one slow silly note, before giving out their final toot.

7. I bet my spirit—once freed—floats over everyone huddled around my failure, before it rises up towards, then through, the ceiling—a feather in reverse, finding its long way back into the wing of the bird that lost it.

OUTSTANDING

This morning I just paid off a credit card—
its balance lingering from college
like a hangover.

Interest rates as swollen as a gut.

I'd like to think I spent all that money
I didn't have on necessities—textbooks,
car repairs, and parking fees.

But it probably all went towards beer.

THIS POEM ISN'T VERY GOOD, BUT IN AN ALTERNATE UNIVERSE SOMEWHERE THERE'S A VERSION OF IT THAT'S MUCH BETTER

In the beginning the car is red,
because the poet wanted to infer passion.

After revising some, they changed their mind—
chose to go with blue to complement the geraniums
mentioned in stanza three.

Later stanza three would be omitted,
because it sounded forced.

Even later still, they decided to be more concise
and left it a mystery altogether—
the car's hue of no real importance
to the poem's heart.

Let its absence perch on the mind
like an extra credit question
at the end of an exam
the test-taker knows won't help
their overall grade.

A draft is its own slice of the multiverse.
Every choice that does not appear in one,

is used perfectly in another.

REAL HUNGER

The dead drum my front door, pressing rotten
palms against the oak as if feeling for a pulse—
some life on the other side.

I can hear their teeth through the walls.

Is it the same for you?
Are we facing similar apocalypses miles apart?

It might be malnourishment talking,
(I've been living off Twinkies)
but all this survival is suffocating me.

My house is a coffin I refuse to rest in.

So please, don't be angry to learn I'd rather face
droves of salivating zombies, than die
never knowing your touch again.

I'll be careful.

I will carry an axe and your name as my war cry,
and show these flesh-eating monsters what real hunger is—
how a kamikaze-heart will not allow itself to be taken
before its mission is complete.

Each decapitation will be a ballad, and every head that drops, an ode.

I will learn to say *I love you* with a forceful swing
so, when we reunite and hold each other, the muscles
in my arms will reveal how often the words kept me alive.

Unless, of course, I'm too late and you've changed.
Now undead, all you'll want is meat.

With my dedications falling on deaf ears,
(if they haven't already been eaten off)
I will speak the only language left you can understand—

human sacrifice.

FIRST KILL

I.

Stop pretending

your lungs can carry the wild weight
of the stampede in your chest.
Reach behind your breath
to find the beast stirring
up all that frenzy
and pull it out

like a fatty, benign tumor.

Hold it to the sky
in ceremonial sacrifice.
Let wind swallow it whole.

Feel weightlessness
for the first time.

II.

Keep busy.

Enroll in space camp.
Take astronaut lessons.
Meet up with the moon
for beers, but order shots
of their best tequila instead.

Really let loose.

The moon gets it.
She has been there.
She knows what it's like
to have rocky lovers crash
into her like fists and leave
behind nothing but holes
the size of regret.

III.

Wake up.
Your head should be the ruins
of a city after an Armageddon—
one far more barbaric than any
found in today's religions.

Ragnarok is a good apocalypse to strive for.

You want to feel
as if there are masses
of battle-fallen Norse gods,
giants, and monsters pulverized
and strewn about your cerebellum.

If it hurts this much,
that is your nervous system
reminding you, you are still alive.

It's easy to forget.

Don't take any aspirin.
Carry the pain like a new tattoo
that reads *survival*,

and ease into the rest of the day.

IV.

When night comes,
go out and find your first kill.

Remember:
you're not looking for love,
just something that tastes like it.

Bring it back to your place, then

      slit its throat,

but don't do it anywhere
near your bed.

That still smells like him.

SECOND COMING, PRIDE PARADE

Drag queens dance around Jesus
like strippers do poles,
and He is doing the sprinkler.

They are atop a float decorated
in a flurry of condom wrappers
and a commanding banner:

Thou shalt practice safe sex.
Madonna's "Like a Prayer"
rings like cherubs' trumpets

and Jesus begins to "vogue."
Everyone whistles and catcalls
as if they were expecting this,

but I am hushed by the miracle—
by the sight of Jesus lifting
His robe high enough to show

us just how good He looks
in sequined, chartreuse heels.
If this is the last judgment

at least we finally know,
What would Jesus do?
Jesus would be fabulous.

ii.

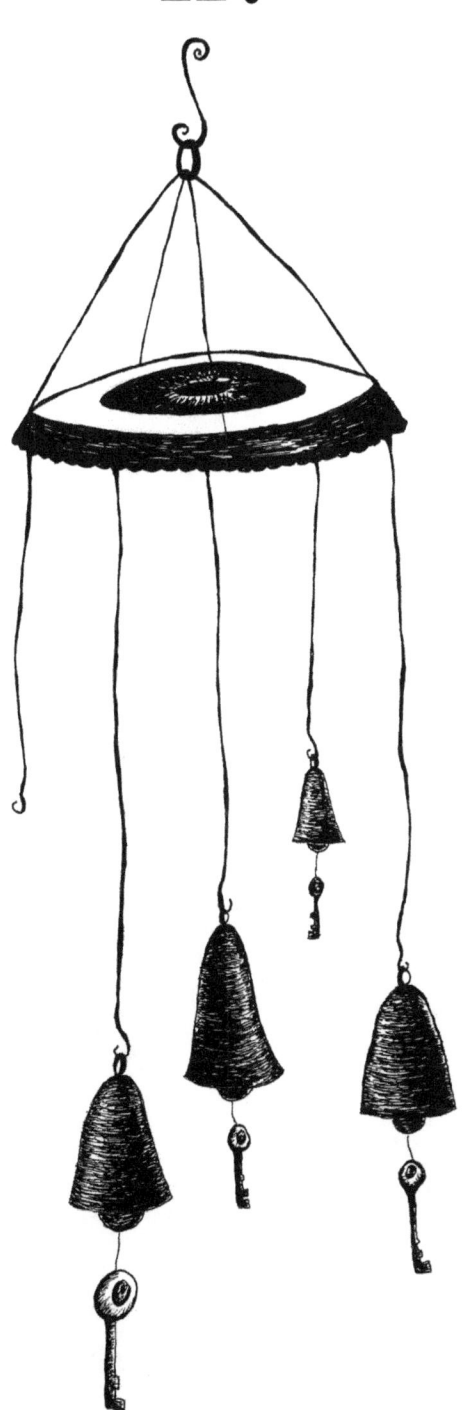

WHAT I SAID TO THE GHOST

I press palms out against the air
like safecrackers put their ears
up to locks, listening for tumblers
to click in perfect succession—
feeling at the static of absence.

My hands are satellite dishes
pointed towards the heavens,
star-bouncing radio waves—
searching empty space
for anything to hold.

Fingers become desperate
letters across a lonely shore—
the word *H-E-L-P* scrawled
in fire, burns to be smothered
by an intangible force.

If I could just touch you,

                I'd believe in everything.

FIRST SESSION

Were I to describe it as gum stuck to the bottom of my shoe that I can't scrape off, would you say I should be grateful it's not quicksand I've stepped in? How about on the days when it's wet concrete, hardening around my feet, trapping me in place? What then?

Is this normal? Can it be fluid? Is anxiety like weight? Is there a target range I should aim for? A chart telling me I'm okay? Or is my just being here a tipped scale?

Where did you get your degree? What was the application process like? Were you carefully selected? Did you get all A's, or the occasional B, even a C? Can I admit knowing your GPA wasn't perfect would make me more comfortable? Is that framed thing hanging on your wall there the ceremonial paper they handed you the day you graduated, or the official diploma sent out months later? Did you grow eager for it, checking the mailbox day after day as though you were waiting on a pair of X-Ray vision glasses? You know the ones, right, the kind offered in old comic book novelty ads and guaranteed to work? Did you believe in their magical science, or doubt?

Are you going to ask me about my childhood? My parents? Could we please save them for another time? Is that an unrealistic request? Am I being too difficult? Would it be all right if today you just taught me to fold anxiety into a less threatening beast—an origami tiger, perhaps? How do I contort my fingers around its size, manage its gnarled shape? Do you think I should be on medication? I've heard meds make you feel as though something alien has infested your brain, rewriting your thoughts with its own chemistry; is any of this true? Have you seen *Invasion of the Body Snatchers*? Did you know there's a fungus that enslaves ants and other insects with mind-control, killing them when they reach an ideal spot for its spores to spread—growing outwards from the inside of its host like a nightmare tree?

Can we explore other options first? Behavioral reconditioning? Controlled breathing techniques or meditation? How about a posthypnotic suggestion? Is that a real thing?

Have you ever been on this side of the couch? Was it easy because you knew what to say? What if my answers aren't good enough or *too* crazy? If I were to make something up or keep something hidden, could you tell? Do people do that often here? Are you trained to spot a liar, to read shifty body language the way hardboiled cops do when trying to crack a perp? You're not going to shine some low hanging ceiling light in my eyes, are you?

Is that jumbo-sized box of Kleenex for when I cry, or do you just have a really bad cold? Do patients cry? If I don't, will it mean there is something wrong with me, and you can't help? Are all these questions, how they itch and tingle under my tongue like an allergic reaction, a usual sensation before our getting started?

How strange is it I keep thinking about those X-Ray glasses, wondering what, if anything, they allow the wearer to see?

WHY I WORE A MAGNETIC EARRING IN THE 7TH GRADE

Because they killed off Superman,
broke Batman's back, and drove
Hal Jordan mad.

90's comic books were getting more extreme,
so I thought I should to do the same
and shoplifted (sort of)

a cubic zirconia magnetic earring,
because I was too embarrassed
to hand my money over for it

to the girl working behind the counter.
(When her back was turned,
I left the cash beside the register and ran.)

I marveled at how the fake diamond
reflected light like a prism;
when the sun hit the stone just right,

I *almost* looked cool. Its faux-gemstone gleam,
my bat-signal I was no longer a boy,
but a teenager ready for…

making dumb decisions.
Magnets pinching skin (over time) hurt,
and eventually, I was concerned

with just how numb my ear had grown—
a poor, pinned mouse in a trap.
When I finally set it free,

a small crater remained.
It took over a day for the dimple to vanish,
but sometimes I feel its impression still there.

A year later and Superman returned
from the grave, farm-boy wholesome as ever,
except for his new haircut—a mullet.

I stopped reading comic books for a while after that.

THE GIRL IN MY POETRY CLASS

defines love in free verse
with such precision
she performs open-heart surgery
on the English Language.

As she reads her poems aloud
their curvy sounding connotations
seduce me
with a modest grace
the way a good wine
excites the palate
without its grapes ever knowing
the power they have.

I imagine every word
is for me alone
an invitation into her world
to lie chest up
and be the patient
she operates on
with perfect intimacy—
I want to be cut open
by her craft
so she can see
how the measure of my heart
beats to the cadence
of her poetry.

But when it comes time
for our class to comment
I always guise my real thoughts
with a clichéd compliment,
and just say, *I liked it.*

My feelings are fantasies
aroused by her writing
I never want ruined by rejection.

I'm all right just knowing
I can look forward to her next poem
to seduce me all over again.

VELCRO

My heart is Velcro
clinging to you tightly.
I've never understood the attraction;
it's a mystery science can explain
in molecular terms, but shouldn't.
All that mumbo jumbo kills the mood.

Besides—
understanding the universe's laws
never gave Newton any wings
to French kiss the sun,
and Icarus, that poor chump,
suffered far worse for trying.

I accept having no control
over this attachment.
I know I'm stuck
on you until someone else
rips us apart, and I'm left
with little annoying pieces of you
fused to me like lint.

FOR WHAT IT'S WORTH

Rather wrestle a rabid hippopotamus in a steel cage match
for an audience of scornful ex-girlfriends. Eat my weight

in pig entrails. Sleep with a thousand Madagascar hissing
cockroaches conducting little bug symphonies every night.

Be the sole survivor of a zombie pandemic. Spontaneously
combust—leaving behind a pile of ash, bits of tooth and bone,

and scorched earth as my only mark on this world. Be ambushed
by ninjas and bludgeoned by nunchucks. Juggle flame engulfed

kittens at gunpoint. Swim in a kiddy pool of afterbirth. Commit
seppuku with plastic picnic ware. Be injected with sodium

pentothal and forced to tell the truth to people I don't like. Suffer
the tedium of a bad poetry reading. Discover Scientology was right.

Have all my organs liquefy. Find the sun is hours from burning
out. I'd rather all this and more than have to see my reflection

in your eyes—how I resemble more a wishbone's losing half
than a man—when I say the words, *I don't love you anymore*,

breaking you like vertebrae.

SUNSET

The moon is multilingual.
He can croon Sinatra's hits in Italian,
recite Neruda in Russian,
and even French kiss in Japanese.

Every evening the moon whispers,
I want you, in a different language,
and seduces the sun
into going down.

EXPANDING UNIVERSE THEORY

A collision between two stars is rare. It is like throwing one marble across a football field and striking a second marble at the far end.

—*Middle school science teacher*

The Sun is lonely.

She is 4.3 light years away from her closest neighbor
and lover, Proxima Centauri, and the distance
is always growing
                      between them.

Physics doesn't think the little star is good enough for his daughter
and pulls the universe at both ends just to keep them apart,
but Proxima still sends her love letters
on the backs of asteroids that read:

    Sunshine,

    One day I will feel your fire.

    XOXO,

    Your Red Dwarf

Science teaches that stars can't wish upon themselves;
there's no magic in it.
So every night they lie awake, never turning their gaze from us,
hoping to catch a glimpse of a shooting spaceship
to cast their wishes on.

Proxima only ever makes one wish—
to touch the sun.
He knows this would end badly for them both,
but doesn't care.
He's a ball of gaseous desire, burning for the kind of love
that will catalyze into new galaxies upon impact.

The Sun adores his recklessness,
how he romanticizes the idea of smashing their atoms together
like kamikazes. She wants to be just as bold—

wants to slip out of her yellow sundress,
put on a leather biker jacket,
blow off all of Physics' rules,
and rewrite her own destiny.

But she can't.
The math of their bodies ever colliding
before they both implode from waiting
grows more impossible
as they are stretched

                                              farther
                                              and
                                              farther
                                              apart.

With only five billion years left,
she knows she'll be dead
before they ever touch—

but this doesn't stop her from smiling
every time she spots a rocket's glow.

Just knowing she, and her lover,
share the same wish, makes
her feel less alone
in all that
cold,

                                        e x p a n d i n g

dark.

THE WORLD WAS SUPPOSED TO END YESTERDAY

but the apocalypse must not have seen the billboards
Harold Camping and his followers put up,
promising Rapture.

Or maybe, it had just forgotten
how to read the Bible as a word problem
and solve for an unknown variable—
the way a poet forgets high school algebra,
after years of never needing it.

I couldn't recite the quadratic formula now,
even if doing so would save us all from the End Times,
but *can* count the metrical feet in a line of poetry.

I don't see how either skill is practical.

Luckily, the world is still here, the apocalypse,
not as punctual as a fringe group of fanatics believed,
so I have time to figure those things out.
Time to do almost anything—

learn to cook the perfect soufflé, to dance
without looking as if I needed medical attention
or find a god, one that doesn't set the alarm
on a doomsday clock.

I've heard scientists are looking for God
in the math of physics—His particles
hiding from us between numbers
like little bugs beneath our floorboards.

I wonder, if we were to ever succeed
in stripping everything back,
would we be disgusted
with what we saw—

billions of God bits crawling
around in the dark,
like we weren't even there.

Would they scatter in the light,
before we tried smashing them
under the worn sole of a boot?

TINY BONES OF YOUTH, LOST

I.

You expect things to be different,
home from college that first time.

Your bedroom turned into a gym.
Treadmill and elliptical machine
replacing boyhood furniture
like new teeth, pushing
the old ones out—

tiny bones of youth, lost.

Perhaps the remodeled kitchen
your mother always wanted,
even though she microwaved
every meal you can remember.

Maybe they even got a dog.

What you're not prepared for
is finding your parents' lube—
the bottle wedged between
two couch cushions like a
misplaced TV remote.

Suddenly the living room
becomes a crime scene.
You play detective, visualize
how it all went down, how
their bodies twisted into lust
as teenagers' do in backseats,
with impulse and fire.

You wish you could shut off
your brain, but there is desire
to understand these people.

Confronting them, you press
questions like a knife to their
throat and beg they not leave
evidence of their sex life
where the guests sit—

they show no shame.

When you get to be our age,
you need a little extra help,
your mother says,

as if she's referring to a new
handrail needed to get in
and out of the shower.

You forget about the lube,
how it's still in your hand,
weightless now compared
to this strange moment,

everything changes.

II.

Your parents come for a visit—

to see you and your fiancé's first home together,
six months after you've already settled in,
and two after the housewarming.

They bring you a lamp.

It is the perfect consolation
prize from a game show
you never could win;

however, you know they expect
answers in the form of questions.

At lunch you ask how your mother's doing.

She shares her sick with you—

informs you of all the pills
doctors have her taking
(and a few they don't)
as though she were gossiping
about the neighbors.

Morphine, a desperate housewife,
your mother likes to sneak tea with.

This won't shock you.

Not the way her calling your father
Daddy over and over again does—

when ordering food,
asking for napkins,
wanting to use the restroom.

Daddy.
                Daddy.
                              Daddy.

You wish it were a sex thing,
this public display of helplessness—
your parents being kinky,
practicing some form of BDSM
while dining out.

But this is not role-play.

This is not your mother cooing
into your father's ear, hinting
he take his Viagra.

It is a fire alarm, deafening.
The backwards tick of a broken clock.
The howl before the crawl,

which finds you unprepared,
itching to lift away, for space,
but there is too much gravity—

and here, everything pulls.

iii.

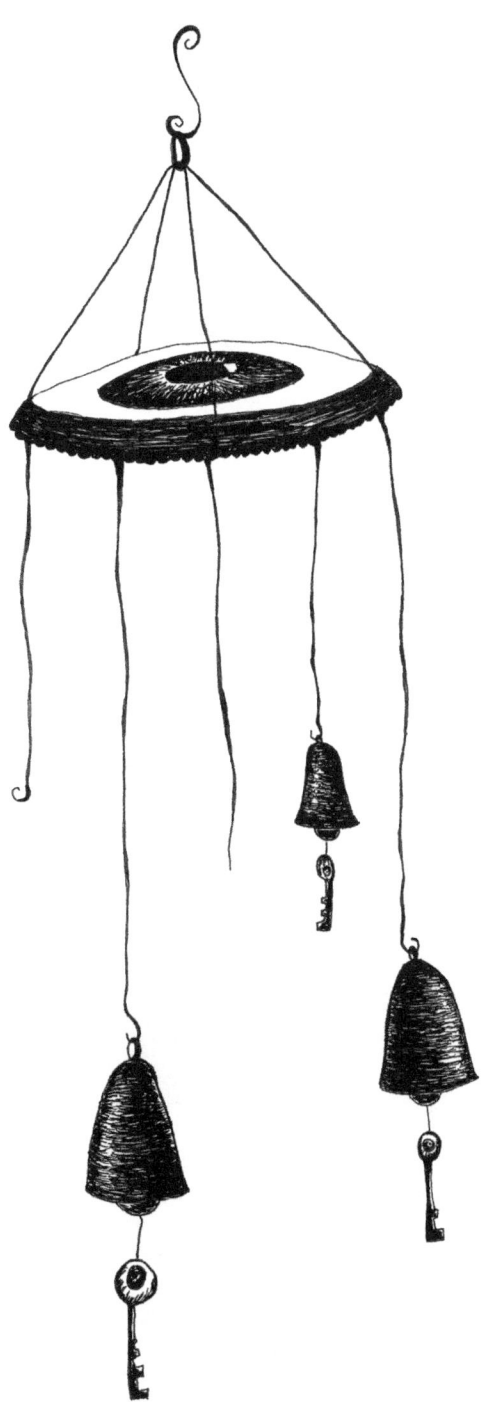

HOMECOMING DANCE

I.

My grandmother is dying.

Fluids swell her lungs like a balloon
expanding under the tap of a sink,
a thin membrane of rubber about to burst—

and I am at the florist

buying a corsage for my date, wishing
flowers meant more at this moment
than promise of condolences to come,
delivered to our door like a pizza
we did not order, nor would care to eat.

The sales clerk asks me which one I want,
I say whichever he thinks will last longest.

II.

Her hospital room is a tightrope we walk,
without any lessons in balance.

It is a muted circus.

The waiting area—a family reunion
of family that rarely sits for a meal together,
and I wonder without her, will we ever again?

Time moves faster than should be allowed.

Before long I have to say *goodbye*,
pick up my date, and try to dance.

III.

My *goodbye* turns into hers.

I am the only one in the room when she leaves.

IV.

It may be selfish, but I do not call for anyone.
The machines will take care of that.

Give me the heavy silence of her gone
over a ruckus of grief.

Soon they rush in like a marching band,
the noise of nurses and doctors, a parade
of apologies and questions.

I don't know the physics of death,
but her hand in mine feels
much lighter now.

V.

At the dance, I force myself
to press close against my date
during slow songs,

but will not hold her hand.

This upsets her, so we sit
and I watch the dance floor moving
as if it were alive, as if when evening ends
and the space clears, it will turn into a ghost.

What are you thinking?

She asks and I want to tell her *everything*—

how I learned today a body, as it dies,
becomes an empty dance floor
in a still and vacant hall.

But all I'm able to do is hold
to the weight of the dead
and re-welcome heavy

silence.

ON THE NIGHT OF MY TEN-YEAR REUNION

I stay home, drinking
from a bottle of scotch,
aged twelve years.

Did you ever want to be more than this? I ask it.

    Sure.

Well what then?

    A Molotov cocktail. How about you?

I don't know. A poet, I guess.

    You and I, kid, we aren't that different, it tells me.

As I take another swig,
I can feel my skin turn to glass,
my booze-soaked guts burning,
and all I want is to throw myself
against this world, shatter and explode—
shatter and explode, into one great fireball
people won't soon forget.

AGAINST BETTER JUDGMENT
The only poem I'll ever write about the McRib

Nothing about you is good for me,
but temptation is a boulder I push uphill;
some days I just want to know
rock bottom and indulge
this hungry curiosity.

I'm done caring what I do
to my body, what stress I put on my heart,
and figure what could it hurt
to finally give in, if only to say,
I've tried what so many others have.

I tell no one my intentions,
certain friends would just want
to talk me off this ledge.

So we meet in secret, late at night,
my bedroom door shut, the world
belonging to just the two of us.

I undress you like a condemned man
does his last meal, but am disappointed
to find you far from what I imagined—
far from any billboard-beauty.

I could—*should*—stop this right now,
but as my hands bring you to my mouth
I convince myself, *looks aren't everything*.

Maybe you'll taste better going down?

You don't. You're lukewarm at best.
I finish as fast as I can.
This is not worth savoring.

After you've gone, regret begins to twist
my guts into a game of cat's cradle,
and guilt becomes a determined inmate
behind my ribcage with a nail file

and a death sentence,
working towards
an impossible freedom.

LIKE A HOT KNIFE THROUGH BUTTER

*We had been talking about our desire
to try sexual bloodletting. It was his knife,
I went first, and it was the most intimate moment
I have ever known.*

—*from a text message*

He kisses her skin and she bleeds
fireflies. Tearing off their wings, he makes
her a pair of earrings and compliments her
on how they bring out the demons in her eyes.

Finally someone who understands me, she thinks
as all the stars waltzing in her head supernova
and begin to break
dance to the drum machine in her chest.

Cutting into his own flesh like an architect,
he designs the means to love her from the inside
out and presses their wounds together like suckerfish.

This is how galaxies are created, he coos,
grinning like a werewolf before a full moon,
like a serial-slasher sharpening his blade,
like Zeus come down the mountaintop
to show her what lightning tastes like.

It tastes like steel,

      is her last thought before sleep.

In the morning he leaves her
with less than when he found her
and a note on the nightstand that reads
Goodbye, in strokes of red.

PRIVATE DANCE

Before the music cues her seduction,
she asks me what I do. I'm not sure why.

Maybe silence before touching a stranger
is unbearable to her, or perhaps she thinks
I'll enjoy it more if we pretend she cares.

I won't. I am here for the friction.

When I tell her I'm a writer, the word
is a shield I brace behind, hoping
she does not advance further.

I hate going into more detail—

how faces become geometry quizzes
I must show all my work for in order
to prove the legitimacy of my answer.

    What do you write?

The song starts, and so do her hips.
A strip club is no place for *ars poetica*,
but she persists.

Her eyes are the ledges men jump from
when desperate to escape what awaits
them at home. I am no exception.

    Poetry.

She leans in close enough to count
the freckles on her breasts,
even in all this dark.

Will you write a poem about me?

> *No.* I say.
> *There's no metaphor in this.*
> *Just skin.*

She presses hers to mine.
Pulse and pause,
pulse and pause.

Like Morse code.
Writes me a novella of touch.
Proves just how wrong I am.

4 HAIKU

1. FOR THE OBSOLETE

Typing two spaces after a period is totally, completely, utterly, and inarguably, wrong.
　　　　　—Slate.com

You will find a friend
in former planet, Pluto—
he doesn't mind space.

2. INSPIRED BY *THE RETURN OF THE LIVING DEAD* (1985)

When girls dance naked
in graveyards, they raise the dead.
Zombie erection.

3. AWKWARD KISS

I'm sorry I burped
when we were making out, but
better than farting.

4. WHEN 17 SYLLABLES ARE NOT ENOUGH

I tip a stripper
with a haiku, and she asks
for more—a sonnet.

I DON'T LIKE STRAWS

in my whiskey.
They insult the integrity
of the alcohol.

So when I order
a Jack on the rocks
don't screw my drink
with a straw.

I want to feel the glass
on my lips
as I choose
whether to sip
sparingly at the stinging nectar,
or heedlessly guzzle down
its burning taste.

I don't want that choice
made for me
by a narrow piece of plastic
distancing me
from my freedom
to choose how swiftly
I escape from this world
where a classless bartender
would ruin a perfectly good drink
with a straw.

SMOLDER

On my way to work, there is a fire
burning along the highway,
flames dancing like a stripper
on a pole made of jet fuel.

Everyone pulls to the shoulder;
they get out of their cars to watch,
to take pictures.

#morningcommute
#destruction
#holyshit

The blaze draws their wonder,

as though Prometheus himself
came down, rubbed the two
sticks together, as if

they never saw a thing burn before.

But I used to scorch—

used to feel my heart swell
so red I thought a devil
lived in my chest, spiking
my poetry like punch at prom.

I'd combust into such protest
people used to stop, gather
and share their stories of ghosts
around my glow, and I'd burn
to bring light to their dark.

That was before a mortgage.

Now I make a manager's salary,
not a writer's singe—suffer
a commute five days a week,
and find glaciers forming under
ribs that once framed a furnace.

Budgets are due and I spend
more time writing emails
than I do poems.

Later the news reports on the fire—
how it was started by a homeless man
trying to cook his dinner.

I hear this and envy him, his hunger,
his need to survive—to spark
flint to feast, despite risk

of smolder and ash.

He knows full well his gamble—
how it could consume,
how even if swallowed up
by that very desire to live,

at least he would go belly full,
torch to his own funeral pyre,
with a parade of onlookers

to see him off, their phones
stretched towards the sky,
cameras flashing brilliant.

#tribute

COVETING THE MAN COVERED IN BURNS

Skin picking is a highly stigmatized and misunderstood disorder, and because of that, many people may not realize their behavior is out of their control—or even that it has a name.
—*Huffington Post*

He touches what is left of his fire-swallowed
skin like an Alzheimer patient might a photo—
tracing fingers over a face he can't remember,
but hopes to one day relearn. There is this air
of gratitude about him, and how he survives
in his body, I will never be able to breathe.
My lungs are two fat fish pulled out of water,
suffocating on something their chemistry cannot
break down. I know what it is to be buried alive.
So confused, I dig release in the wrong direction,
clawing my own flesh, searching for a better me,
somewhere closer to the bone. Shame pushes up
like magma, hot and red, then cools and hardens.
When I touch these scars, I want only to forget.

HOME REMEDY

Our grandmother rubbed Aloe vera on everything—
grew so much of it in her backyard,
you'd think she was stockpiling for an apocalypse.

We'd come to her with cuts and scrapes, bruises and bug bites,
and with all the medical know-how of a gardener,
she'd snip a leaf and press its bleeding end to our wound
like she were putting a cigarette out against skin.

Then, as if she had sawed a man in half
and brought him back together again,
she would smile and say *All better*.

The parlor tricks did not stop there.

She'd knead it into temples if we had a headache.
A sore throat, and we'd be forced to gargle with it.
She even thought it could cure pinkeye—
smeared the goop above our cheekbones like cold cream.

We always joked if ever we lost an arm or leg,
she'd just slather the bloody stump with it
and expect the limb to reappear.

But years later, after all our wounds did indeed heal,
when death came for her like a punchline,
and doctors said nothing could be done—
the idea was no longer funny.

We asked ourselves, and sometimes still do:

What would it hurt to believe in magic,
to paint a mural of miracle on a body?

PLAYING THE GAME *WOULD YOU RATHER*, YOU ASK

Death by drowning, or by fire?

Neither.
I wish for a third option:

> to fall,
> like a rock from space.

Let me crater this world
and smash blood and bone
with dirt and gravel.

Let our molecules kiss hard.

Have it be messy.

Have it take forensic experts
to identify the body;

and even then, make it impossible
to find every scattered bit—
for them to bury anything
resembling a man.

I want my impact to last—

the way a tree grows
around the valley of a name
carved deep in its trunk.

As for those brief moments
before the end, you ask me:

Would I be afraid?

but falling is merely flying
in the direction of down.

I'd enjoy my last breaths,
a wind-kissed bird, hairs
on my arms transformed—

tiny feathers,
feasting on sky
until, so full,

        I sank to the earth.

iv.

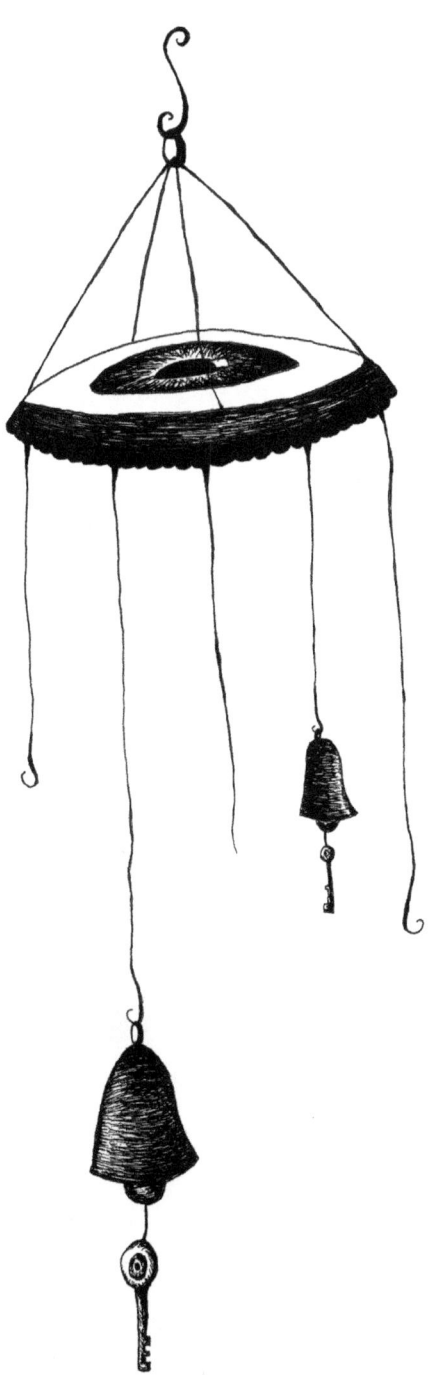

SURVIVING A MOUNTAIN LION ATTACK, AS INSTRUCTED BY EHOW.COM

1. Mountain lions tend to avoid people. If one is approaching, give it a chance to escape.

I try ignoring you from across the bar. I know you are trouble by the way you hold the neck of your beer.

2. Look the lion in the eyes if it continues to approach.

You come over and say you want some air. It is neither invitation, nor proper greeting. I am confused whether or not to follow, but something about your eyes say *yes*.

3. Make loud noises. Showing your teeth and growling may help.

I offer my name. You don't tell me yours. I smile, hoping to pull it out of you like a loose tooth, but you, all fangs and flirtation, know how to play with your food.

4. Make yourself appear larger. Remove your jacket and stretch it overhead.

You look cold. I offer my coat, but you extend your arms as though you want to share our body's heat. This is you sizing me up.

5. Stand up straight and stick out your chest.

Convinced you have a good inch over me, we compare height as if we're kids teasing each other over who stands in front of whom in line. You tell me to keep still, and then come in real close so we are chest to chest and lips to lips.

6. Pull children close and, if possible, put a small child on your shoulders to increase size. If there are other adults, stand close.

There is no one around. Certainly no children here. We are alone in this wild.

7. If you feel you can retreat, back away slowly, remembering to never turn your back to the animal.

Instinct tells me to run, but I don't think I'd get very far on foot before you'd have me pinned.

8. Use anything within reach as a weapon and try to avoid bending over to get at it. If you have a bicycle, hold it as a shield.

If *only* I had a bicycle.

9. If no weapon is available, target an eye and jab it with your thumb (people who have done this have been successful).

You are a ceiling coming down on me; I press my fingers against your skin to slow your course.

10. Yell *lion*, *cougar*, or something specific instead of just *help*.

I whisper *mercy*, because I still don't know your name. Biting my ear, you tell me my talking ruins your appetite—then something powerful takes me by the throat so I have no words. I make my final prayers, silent.

INTANGIBLE

I.

At twelve years old I was in love with a girl
I could never touch.

Kitty Pryde was everything
a nerdy preteen dreams of—
next-door-sweetheart-sexy,
computer wiz, and (my mother
would have been so proud) Jewish.

She was also a ninja with a pet purple
dragon. I'd picture the loyal beast,
perched, guarding over our bicycles
outside the arcade where we'd spend
quarters as if they were kisses—
as if we would never run out.

Most importantly, she was an X-Man.
A mutant. Born different. An outcast.
What misshapen, near-sighted, metal-mouthed
twelve-year-old boy wouldn't fall for her kind
of special? Her power, to phase through walls

(and my heart), to walk through anything—
be a ghost, float on air, untouchable.
I thought, *How astonishing, such freedom.*

II.

Thirty-three and I've learned to love women
of flesh, not fiction—

have found romance beyond the splash
pages of comic books, and understand
how the real thing is much better than
any twelve-year-old boy can imagine.

I know now how necessary the tactile is—
skin to skin like rain to earth,
heart to heart like bones to body.

III.

My love, now, is as much the sharp hard
glass of a mirror as she is the smoke—

Our bodies can bind to the other
the way concrete gives release
to roots' push, and yet at times,
my hand passes right through
the illusion of her presence—

as if the molecules of her heart
have acquired the talent to phase
on command when put in danger.

As we grow in this relationship,
as conversations turn to last name
changes and children, I feel she is

becoming more intangible.

I saw her the other day, fading
into an apparition, weightless,
walking a tightrope of air,
before vanishing into the wall.

There is no freedom in this.

And I wish, more than anything,
I was twelve again, easily astonished,
perfectly content loving that which

I could never touch.

HOW YOU SPEND YOUR SUMMER VACATION

1. You start by changing the spelling of your name; replacing the *C* with a *K*, because going into 8th grade, you want things to be different. You want to kick the ass of any bully who gets in your face—to do it in front of a crowd, to knock the jerk down like a piñata, their teeth scattering like hard candy at the feet of cheering kids. You believe this new consonant is what will transform a boy into a man.

2. One Friday night, your father rents *The Rocky Horror Picture Show* on VHS, and you have to leave the room when watching it with him. The next morning when he goes golfing, you return to the film. You fast forward to certain scenes—watch and rewind, watch and rewind. You study the push of Susan Sarandon's chest against the hands of an unsure creature, as if there will be a test on it later.

3. Having nearly failed math, your parents force you to retake it in summer school. You spend six weeks learning how numbers fit together to tell perfect stories on the page, and actually begin to like algebra. You also meet a girl in the class named Desiree, pass notes back and forth, and try not to misspell her name. Desire. She calls you every night and tells you about the hand jobs she's given to freshmen in high school—how she holds them like a dripping, sticky ice cream cone. You do not believe a word she says, but her voice tugs your skin in a new way. You become a good listener.

4. An arcade opens a few blocks away and it is magic. Pinball becomes a drug. You barter chores for quarters and spend whole afternoons trying to make them last. When they run out, you return home, as fast as you can, and ask if there are any dirty dishes to be done.

5. One afternoon in July, your mother takes you out for frozen yogurt and asks if you've had a chance to read the book she bought you—*What Is Happening to My Son's Body?* You push your plastic spoon deep into the bowl in front of you as though you're digging an escape tunnel. You then lie, shaking your head no. *Well, when you do,* she says, *and have questions, let me know.* Later, you throw the book away in a dumpster down the alley and tell her you lost it.

6. You enjoy spending weekends at your father's, because he leaves you alone for long periods of time while he golfs, and keeps a bottle of margarita mix in his fridge. Every so often you take a swig from it, careful not to take too much. Each sip makes you feel cool and dangerous and ready for adulthood; you're certain you are getting buzzed. It will take some time before you figure out what you're drinking isn't alcohol—just sugar and lime juice.

7. The last week of summer, Desiree invites you to her birthday party. You trace your twelve-year-old fingers over the gold embossed number *10*, and the two little letters that follow it, *PM*. This will be the latest you have ever been to a girl's house. If life were a game of pinball, this moment would fall somewhere between a tri-ball and a free-play.

8. You kiss a girl for the first time, during a game of spin the bottle. The two of you are pushed into a hall closet, barely able to see one another. It smells of old wool coats, cedar hangers, and adolescent sweat. On the other side of the door, there are cheers and someone counting down, but for you, time quiets and stops. You lean into her with careful courage, like a blindfolded boy swinging a stick at a hanging papier-mâché beast—a boy who is starved for its sugar-spoils, for its sweet insides to rain down over him, victorious. However, she turns the tables and makes you *her* party favor. Her lips shatter ribs. Her mouth makes you forget the spelling of your own name. And after those thirty long

seconds are over, you realize it is you who has busted open and spilled out—who has just lost something you cannot get back.

SQUEEZE

It's about the work.

—Lee Strasberg

There are those who make a living extracting
venom from the world's most lethal snakes—
they squeeze their glands until poison squirts
from hollow fangs, collecting vials of the stuff

like homemade preserves. Using only a stick
and their bare hands, they coerce the creatures
ever so routinely—as though the job were no
more dangerous than an oil change, or pouring

a cup of coffee. I am jealous of their apparent
ease, and of the poet who can write just like this.
Creativity merely a gland, the slightest pressure
can arouse—the perfect order of words no harder

to come by than a snake bite. It has taken me
two whole days just to conjure that last stanza,
and it's not even that impressive. I swear my
imagination is a constrictor, with unrelenting

grip. It coils over and around my entire body.
The more I give struggle, the tighter it clasps,
until bones break, blood leaks, and I asphyxiate
on all the unborn words trapped in my throat.

FREE ASSOCIATION

*I've had a shitty day;
work has been a real kick
to the nuts*, I tell my therapist.

He tries to switch subjects on me,
asks about my upcoming wedding:
When is it, again?

In a couple weeks, I say.
Wow, that's soon, he responds.
Then he pauses for a long moment,

as if he's searching for something
profound and therapeutic
to share with me, like hope.

I imagine his advice: *true love
is a cup to protect your balls.*
But instead, he wants to know:

Have you seen Rosemary's Baby?
I remain silent, really trying
to get the connection he is making

between my nuptials and a film
about a pregnant woman
giving birth to the Antichrist.

When I don't answer right away,
he laughs, realizes how strange
his association must sound,

explains the psychedelic scene
where Mia Farrow is raped
by Satan and shouts:

This is no dream.
This is really happening.
His explanation doesn't help

convince me he's any less odd,
but I do laugh—the kind of laugh
that exorcises demons.

That devil I've been carrying
around, evicted—the pain
in my groin, gone.

WHEN MY THERAPIST SHARES HIS POETRY WITH ME

In the evenings I teach a poetry workshop.
One student is a chiropractor,
but I have never considered
requesting she realign my spine
in between critiques.

Imagine it—
me, face down on the floor,
her hands finding their way
along vertebrae, as I work
out the kinks riddling her words.
A cacophony of cracks and pops,
stifling the clarity of my edits.

So when my therapist shares his poetry
with me during one of our sessions,
I wonder if he's crossing a line.

Or if perhaps it's not so uncommon
for him to have his opinion solicited
in someone else's office,
when *he's* being charged by the hour,
when *he's* vulnerable and seeking answers
only their expertise can give.

As he reads his poem aloud,
as it lunges from his mouth—
a crazed bungee jumper too excited
to take caution before the leap,
to be certain there's enough space
between the end of the rope and the earth,

I become more and more uncomfortable,
as though it is my own body at risk here.

But when he finishes, it is *his* silence
that dangles its limbs in front of us,
and for once, he is the bridge
uncertainty hurtles from,
while I am the ground
it fall towards.

There is power in such inevitability.

He asks for my thoughts,
wants to know about his trees,
and the dirt and the red sky,
how his red sky lives
in balance with it all—

how everything lives in balance.

I don't like Nature poetry,
but understand his intent
behind describing the soil as bricklike,
yet soft as powdered sugar,
in showing that which is suspended
above is the same below.

Awaiting my response, his eager
inkblot eyes beg for meaning—
some small validation his words
aren't crazy, that they make sense
to someone, trained, like myself.

I see the reflection in the symmetry,
but choose not comment on it.
Instead, I simply tell him:

I think your poem is working.

PRIORITIES

Describing the discipline
we would need post-MFA,
our professor, as if reading

stats off his favorite player's
baseball card, loved to share
how Wanda Coleman would

wake up at 4 AM every day,
hours before work, to write—
to survive the sun's swallow.

She was a great earthquake
of a poet, able to push past
bedrock at any ungodly hour.

It is 5 AM and I am recalling
this while hitting my alarm's
snooze button with the grace

of a blind bomb squad, until
I finally just reset it to go off
again at 7 AM. *Enough time*

to get something on the page,
I convince myself—then settle
back into sleep, and on the fact

how I may only ever be a mild
tremor of a poet. Never great—
but certainly more well-rested.

STARSTUFF

This poem wants to be read
like a suicide note as serious as lightning
in the backyard of your heart.

This poem wants to seduce you
like a short black dress, no visible panty line,
and too much spiced rum.

It wants to fist fight your nightmares
like John Wayne in old Westerns.
This is a barroom brawl poem—
a broken-beer-bottle-jagged-glass poem,
a switchblade itching to be sprung poem.

This poem wants to bruise egos
and cut the wings off from the shoulders of angels.
It's dangerous like that.

Not Michael Jackson, 1991 "Dangerous"

This poem wants absolutely nothing to do with Michael Jackson…

Besides that last reference.

This poem wants to be irrelevant and play the fool.
It wants to be a banana-cream-pie-in-the-face-gag.
It wants to be the accidental kick to the groin
that is always funny to watch.
This poem wants to make you laugh milk out your nose.

This poem wants to sing music like a jukebox
full of old 45's that sound the way mom's apple pie tasted
when you'd watch Saturday morning cartoons
and not your cholesterol.

This poem wants to tell bedtime stories you can dream to.
It wants to play checkers with your subconscious
and double jump
                                      all
over
                the   place.

This poem doesn't like rules.
This poem wants to catalyst.
This poem wants to be the start of something big.

This poem wants to bang.

This poem wants to shoot you so full of starstuff
your lungs expand into spaceships,
take off,
and leave you gasping.

Then this poem
will nestle itself behind your ribcage
with an ease suggesting that is where it has always belonged,
and you'll be able to breathe again.

ONE MAN'S TRAINWRECK IS ANOTHER'S GOLDEN GOOSE

Give me a groom's gay lover outing him in front of the guests
as the priest asks for objections, or a guilt-ridden bride confessing

she's really her fiancé's long lost fraternal twin carrying their baby.
Show me Jesus up on a giant cross coming unhinged and falling

flat on a homely maid of honor. Have her arms flailing and legs
kicking about from under her savior just before she loses

consciousness, crushed by the good Lord's might and Vatican oak.
Rose petals from her bouquet scattered like piñata candy—

everybody in a puzzled hush. I want to bear witness to total chaos
in the face of matrimony and have a good long laugh at its expense.

But with my luck, my own nuptials will be the very disaster
I've dreamt of watching. Perhaps my wife-to-be will suffer

food poisoning and projectile vomit chunks of underdone meat
as though her gut were a catapult. Or maybe some jilted ex,

like some irradiated gargantuan sea monster, will wreck havoc
on the ceremony and my happiness by announcing she faked it

every time. And my dear, sweet fiancé, a vision in her dress,
as lovely as a sunrise after a stormy night, will turn and say,

It's all right, baby. We all have a past. In fact, I used to be a man.
Friends and family might gasp, while some may even chuckle

at the unfortunate timing of this revelation, but we'd still kiss—
two folds of a fortune cookie, pressed together around one future.

V.

CONFESSIONS OF A RETIRING MAGICIAN
for Ryan & Jamie

I used to perform vanishing acts nightly
and considered myself a professional escape artist.
Straitjackets fit as comfortably as a good woman—
I never met one I couldn't walk away from.
Sure, I had to dislocate certain body parts from time
to time, but it was worth it to not feel tied down
by any one girl. And I've hypnotized whole crowds
of women into thinking they were hummingbirds,
Marilyn Monroe, or more amazing than the word
abracadabra. I've taken volunteers from the audience,
a different girl every night, and had them convinced
they were in the spotlight, when really I was the star
of the show. After a while I got so tired of faking it.
I couldn't levitate from rock bottom even with wires
hooked to my sleeves. Figured it was time to give
it all up when sawing myself in half came easy,
because I was already in pieces.

Then you came around.
Now I find myself laying all my cards on the table.
You've turned every suit in the deck into a heart
and for the life of me I can't figure out how
you did it. I thought mine was an empty top hat,
but you've been pulling rabbits and flowers
and fish bowls from it since the day we met, proving
I am just an illusionist. You're the real magician
able to suspend disbelief. Teach me that trick
and in return I'll show you my very last one.
Pick a card. Any card. Don't put it back in the deck.
Instead hold the card flat in your palm
so everyone can see it's a heart, and watch
as I don't disappear.

YOU'RE A GOOD ZOMBIE, CHARLIE BROWN

It started with Woodstock—some mutated strain
of bird flu. His first victim, Pig Pen, tasted terrible,
but the hunger was just too overpowering to care

about good hygiene. Next peanut down was Marcie—
cleaning her glasses, she never saw it coming. Upon
infection she went straight for Peppermint Patty.

You always hurt the ones you love, sir. When they
came for Charlie Brown, he thought *good grief*—
wondered if MetLife had him covered as both girls

undressed the flesh from his bones. This was not
the threesome he wanted. His sister, Sally, heard
his screams across the hall and cried hysterically.

Cried not for herself, but because she knew who
she would go to when she turned. But Linus,
not wanting to go out like that, did what he must—

took his blue blanket, fashioned a noose around
his neck, and hung himself from the ceiling fan.
Sally scratched for days at a door to a quiet room.

Snoopy showed more courage and jumped atop
his dog house to take aim at Charlie Brown's
half-eaten head. Though by the time he realized

his dogfights with Red Baron were all pretend,
it was too late. Blood splattered everywhere—
Snoopy became invisible beside his red home.

Lucy, seeing there was money to be made
in times of a zombie apocalypse, increased
her cost for psychiatric help to 15 cents, but

soon regretted it when a reanimated Snoopy
came for her brain. She was always terrified
of his kiss—more so now—tried outrunning

him, but it wasn't long before he was lapping
her cheek with his tongue, then chewing it off
with his teeth. Her only consolation was that

in death she finally could have what she wanted
in life—Schroeder, all to herself, away from his
toy piano. She ate his fingers first, like taquitos.

Through it all he continued to play—banged
his bloody stumps against the tiny ivory keys
until every bit of Beethoven left his body.

The sole survivor of the group, Franklin, who,
having no anxiety or obsessions to distract him,
saw this horror show coming and escaped, long

before his friends noticed he'd gone. He refused
to be killed off that way—consumed like cliché,
becoming just another monster, same as them.

FOR ALL INTENSE AND PORPOISES, THIS POEM IS A MISTAKE

English was their second languish

—Brendan Constantine

I could careless
that it isn't vary good.
I didn't have tim to edit.

Please accent this apology.
My spellcheek is is broken.
I need those red, squiggly limes.

Ginsberg was write—
fist thought, best though.
Why argue wit greatness?

I'm advent guard
and inspired by Dodo.
You just don't udderstand.

I saw another poet do tit,
so it seemed like a god idea.
Although his was probably batter.

SHE CALLS IT WASTEFUL WHEN I LEAVE FOOD ON MY PLATE, AND I CALL IT POLITICS

*What about all the starving children
in third world countries?*
she'll ask me, outraged by a few stray fries.
I assure her, *I do my part*.

I order a tall from Starbucks,
never supersize anything,
and only ever make two trips
at an all-you-can-eat buffet,

because I try to not force food down
when feeling the least bit full.
I don't see how stuffing my gut
to the point of discomfort does anything
to help poor, famished children.

But when I go to my favorite sushi bar
and the chef gives me extra sashimi,
doubles my order of unagi, and offers up
a spicy scallop hand roll—

all for free,

I can't *not* eat
every
last
bite
to show my thanks.

(Also, I fear his generosity would stop, if I didn't.)

I am grateful for his giving me more
and more, unasked, despite how I hold
my wretched stomach like some creature
is gestating within, to show I've had enough.

And maybe that right there is the reason
our country is obsessed with its Big Gulps,
SUVs, and 128 gigabyte iPhones—

why the Bible Belt was traded in
for an elastic waistband.

America's belly so full of gratitude, it's about to burst.

BIGFOOT'S TO-DO LIST

☐ Go for a long morning run. Remember this year's resolution to trim your waistline—it's embarrassing to have feet so big, and not be able to see them.

☐ Meet the bears down by the creek for a hearty breakfast of salmon, wild berries, nuts, and grubs.

☐ On your way back, swing by the campgrounds. Make a few scattered tracks in the fresh mud. Give the people what they want—what they have come to expect. Never mind that the story of you has become larger than you feel.

☐ Avoid being photographed in focus.

☐ Floss.

☐ Get to work. Shoot another email to Universal about syndicating *Harry and the Hendersons*. Compose a letter to Jack Link's Beef Jerky expressing your anger over their "Messing with Sasquatch" advertising campaign and their insulting representation of your species' intelligence. Begin outlining memoir, *Big Feet, Little Life*.

☐ Nap. Dream of a pedicure.

☐ Come dusk, while campers are boozing around their fires telling ghost stories, jostle tents, rustle around in the shrubs, defecate in their cookware. Cause alarm and intrigue, without revealing your true self. Try to enjoy it. Don't think about how the word *legend* is a steel-jawed trap around your ankle—how if you could, you'd gnaw at it, clean through bone to escape. Before you leave, steal something.

☐ Return home in time to watch *The Tonight Show*. Pour yourself a drink and ease into your evening. Keep from gloomy thoughts. Rather, consider the fascination you provided the world today. Put *be grateful* on tomorrow's "to-do" list.

THE SILVER BRIDGE

Many people thought Mothman was responsible for the fall of the Silver Bridge, connecting West Virginia with Ohio on December 15, 1967 during rush hour traffic. Others said he was trying to warn people of the upcoming tragedy.

—*Coast to Coast* Radio Program

Concrete and steel turned wreckage.
A modern day Atlantis
at the bottom of the Ohio River.

My sunken tragedy, a promise
your strange presence delivered
like an unwanted bouquet
from a sorry ex, whose love
was more fist than open palm.

Or worse yet, a severed ear,
tucked between pages of the morning paper—
a mobster's warning to *listen well*.

When folks started swapping
their sightings of you
like fishing stories:

a wingspan the size of a pickup
...no wait...
a stretch limo

I knew disaster wasn't far behind.

The devil-red glow of your eyes—
foreshocks to the collapsing
of my outstretched body.

I know you shouldn't shoot the messenger,
but it's hard not to point that barrel at you,
when they built a statue in your honor,
as if you were more town founder
than angel of death.

My name did not even appear
on their engraved plaque,
and I fear what I am to become—
a forgotten ruin.

Tell me, do you carry any guilt
on your winged back, is the weight
of it heavy enough to impress my name
forever on your flesh?

Do the letters spell out a canyon of regret?

FROM THE LOCH, TO THE MONSTER

Thank you for hiding yourself in my body—
for letting only me in on the mystery of you.
I have kept silent and dark for so long, that
the fish are all blind and I cannot recall what
color ever was. But you, my sweet creature,
were worth it. You've been banshee's song.
Sonar-splendor, humming under skin. How
many have come now to put ear to my water,
to my murky heart? I'm no longer an empty
lake of wanting. Tourists, scientists, even
skeptics whisper my name like incantation,
hoping if it is said just so, you will appear
from obscured depths—a riddle's answer.
Now is the time for the reveal, for release.

This world needs reminding the fantastical
exists, even if unseen. Give more than fin
or neck, blurred in photo—your fingerprint
smeared from the scene. Show hard proof
you are no driftwood, wake or hoax, but
tangible anachronism refuged in shadow.
Let your myth become fact become fame.
Feel no guilt or worry—this is not so much
a breakup, as it is a breakout. You deserve
the limelight, and I the freedom to relearn
sky. How I've wished for sun to skip over
my surface like a stone, then sink beneath
so I might shine from bottom up. Finally
brilliant, able to be legend all on my own.

CONTROLLED CRASH

My hands are glass windowpanes,
shaking from anxious thunder.
I'm certain they'll crack, shatter,
as I give the receptionist
a copy of my insurance,
presenting it like a failing kid
does their report card.

She does not acknowledge
this shame, tells me I must answer
a questionnaire before my first session
with the therapist, and asks I be
as honest as possible:

*Do you have a tendency towards
compulsive behavior? Excessive
or senseless worrying?
Frequent periods of déjà vu?
(Frequent periods of déjà vu?)*

I do feel as if I've been here before,
in a rerun of a dream where nerves
sabotage sleep, taking a test for a class
I don't remember ever attending.

I hide my panic like shoplifted gum.

In the corner of the room,
there is a TV airing breaking news—
a commercial jet has crash-landed
at San Francisco airport.
They show its great metal bones,
smoldering atop the runway—
a funeral pyre for any belief
we belong in the sky.

They're still trying to understand
what causes such a whale to fall.
We are all trying to understand.

A pilot goes on to explain,
how in flight school they learn
all landings are nothing more
than a controlled crash.

Sitting here this first time,
waiting and panic-stashed,
with a storm of apprehension
rattling around my ribs,

I realize *this* is my landing—
find comfort when I look
down at my hands and see
they are still whole.

3 BILLION BEATS

*With only a limited number of heartbeats,
it is best not waste them on exercise.*

*—Overheard conversation between two men
in a retirement home*

He's right. It *is* best not to throw precious beats away
on machinery and repetition like some Nike-endorsing
Sisyphus, forcing your muscles to tear and heal,
tear and heal, in a room that smells of iron,
rubber, and Gatorade.

Lay your heart to waste on life—
Reserve at least a billion thumps for making love,
setting some aside for just sex—dizzy and lusty.
Exert a couple mil on eating—chewing taffy, biting
into chili peppers on dares, having a slice of pizza,
and then another and another until your gut swells
with grease and cheese, or enjoying a Thanksgiving
feast more than once a year. Indulge tens of thousands
trying every flavor of ice cream twice. Drink. Spend
a good deal on pitchers of beer with friends, bottles
of wine over romantic dinners, and shots of whiskey
for when times are hard, as they often can be.

Splurge half a billion doing *anything* foolish—
investing in real-estate on the moon, reenacting
the battle of Gettysburg with silly string, kidnapping
lawn gnomes for a ransom of jellybeans, or sending
exotic postcards inscribed *wish you were here*
to unknown addressees, are all good uses of a heartbeat.
Use up a bunch just being able to laugh at yourself.
Devote a multitude to doing something creative. Write

poetry. Dedicate hundreds of millions and millions
to crafting a few great poems, and even more heartbeats
toiling over the rest you never gave up on.

If by the end of your life you find you have some to spare,
don't squander them in a fitness gym trying to avoid Death
like he's some creditor calling about your overdue balance.
Rather save your very last beats for the words,

thank you, thank you, thank you.

THE FIRST TIME I SAW SNOW FALL WAS ALSO THE ONLY TIME I EVER

heard our father carry any guilt, sharp
and hard, in his throat, like a chicken bone,
when he called to tell me how you died—
pills—in your sleep. *Miracles do happen*,
I thought, as outside, the ground disappeared,
turned soft, became something new. A blank
page. There were questions I could've asked—
designed to hurt, to cleave his heart open,
to better understand how a father lets a son
go, long before he *must*. Instead, I took
my rage, waited for the snow to form hands
large enough to catch a collapsing body,
then fell, like a devil trying to grow back
its wings, into all that blinding white.

ACKNOWLEDGMENTS

Grateful acknowledgment is made to the editors of the following publications in which these poems have previously appeared:

Bank Heavy Press: "Real Hunger"
Cadence Collective: "Home Remedy" & "The First Step to Treating Mental Illness"
East Jasmine Review: "The First Time I Saw Snow Fall, Was also the Only Time I Ever"
FreezeRay Poetry: "You're a Good Zombie, Charlie Brown"
Incandescent Mind: "Coveting the Man Covered in Burns"
In-flight Literary Magazine: "First Session," "Playing the Game *Would You Rather*, You Ask"
Litnivorous: "From the Loch, to the Monster"
RipRap: "Velcro"

"I Don't Like Straws" & "The Girl in My Poetry Class" appear in *Carving in Bone: An Anthology of Orange County Poetry* (Moon Tide Press, 2007)

"Intangible" appears in *Multiverse: An Anthology of Superhero Poetry of Superhuman Proportions* (Write Bloody, 2014)

"Reverse" appears in *A Poet is a Poet No Matter How Tall III: Short Poems Ain't Got Nobody to Love* (For the Love of Words, 2016)

Thank you:

Sara Khayat and the Paper Plane Pilot crew for publishing this collection; it feels wonderful to give these poems such a good home. Alisha Attella and Nancy Lynée Woo for their trusted critiques and valuable edits. Danielle Mitchell for helping me see how these poems fit together, in a way I never thought to look. Half Off Books for their space to host readings and workshops, and to all the poets who have taken workshop from me—I learn as much from you, if not more, than you do from me. Dennis Gowans for helping me "control crash." I think I'm starting to stick the landing. Friends and family, for their encouragement and support—especially Rob Sturma, Laurel Ann Bogen, G. Murray Thomas, Michael Miller and Moon Tide Press, Ray and Christi Lacoste, and Zachary and Tammy Locklin. And of course, my wife, Katie O'Shaughnessy, for being my blowtorch in a candle factory.

Eric Morago is a two-time Pushcart Prize nominated poet who believes performance carries as much importance on the page, as it does off. Currently he hosts a monthly reading series, teaches writing workshops, and serves as an associate editor for the online literary journal, *FreezeRay Poetry*. Eric is the author of *What We Ache For* (Moon Tide Press) and has an MFA in Creative Writing from California State University, Long Beach. He lives with his wife and three dogs in Los Angeles, California.

www.ingramcontent.com/pod-product-compliance
Lightning Source LLC
Chambersburg PA
CBHW071141090426
42736CB00012B/2190